DIVINE
FOOTSTEPS

DIVINE
FOOTSTEPS

Thy way is in the sea, and
thy path in the great waters
PSALM 77:19

JOHN METCALFE

THE PUBLISHING TRUST
Church Road, Tylers Green, Penn, Buckinghamshire.

Printed and Published by
John Metcalfe Publishing Trust
Church Road, Tylers Green,
Penn, Buckinghamshire

—

—

First Published 1972
Reprinted 1975
Second Edition 1989

—

ISBN 1 870039 21 1. 2nd edition
(ISBN 09502515 1 8. 1st edition)

—

CONTENTS

DIVINE FOOTSTEPS

I

The Lord's Feet

IT is a great thing to appreciate his feet; indeed every limb and feature of his blessed body has been lovingly cherished in the framework of affectionate words and sound doctrine by the Holy Ghost. In one sense those feet reveal everything, because everything takes its place in relation to his feet.

There are things one should consider about the feet of the Lord. The first is, that he has feet at all! Yet this is a point—so obvious in itself—that is to those who are dulled by long familiarity with religious and biblical things too easily overlooked: thus its pungency and the sharpness of the tremendous truths that it conveys are lost by the effect of habitual complacency smothering the earnestly seeking spirit of freshly awakened expectancy.

1

To thoughtfully contemplate that the Lord has feet at all is to marshal momentous criteria in massive and stupendous proportions, at once pregnant with awesome mysteries and attendant by staggering conclusions: that he possesses feet proper to his body predicates incarnation, postulates assumption, argues two natures but manifests one person. To state that he has such limbs who is the Eternal, who has both the nature of God and of man, yet in the unity of his being can at once address the Father as God, receive worship from men and angels, can speak of God the Holy Ghost issuing forth from his person, yet declare that of himself he could do nothing, can stand on earth and say that he is in heaven—what majestic mysteries are thus supported by such humble limbs.

That he has such members at all brings forth the most tremendous truths in the whole new testament: the fundamentally greatest truth of the faith is the revelation of the unknown deity in the person of the Son. Law hid Jehovah, but grace and truth in Jesus Christ revealed him as one God —Hear, O Israel: the LORD our God is one LORD.—but three persons, in the everlasting bonds of eternal relations in the unity of divinity: three divine persons in one Godhead, Three in One and One in Three; three distinct persons in one essence: one essence in three distinct persons: and those divine persons eternally in the relationship of Father, Son and Holy Spirit. This is the most important truth in the whole bible, in heaven, on earth, in time, and through eternity—it is that without which all else falls to the ground—yet this truth would never have been revealed but for that body which is based upon his feet.

He now has feet! Who was spirit from eternity past, who came out of heaven's glory into the world, out of eternity into time, outwith deity into humanity, the invisible intangible, the eternal inscrutable, the Almighty, the only wise God; he took such feet in incarnation as had not yet been properly formed, was made of a woman and was duly born with tiny infant's limbs perfect and unmarked. But these grew and walked in the way prepared; matured and progressed in the foreordained path: to the cross. There they pierced this man's feet—feet now mature, calloused now, yet so vulnerable before the percussive drive of the nails. These feet were seen in resurrection—they held him by the feet—these feet were eternally marked by the wounds; these feet, flesh and bones, were seen ascending. *These feet exist!* One day, whether in our earthly lifetime or not, but in the resurrection at the last day, all shall bow before them in awe, perforce or in an ecstasy of love...... .

O blessed feet of Jesus! Mary sat at his feet. Consider also the creation of Jesus' feet: made of a woman by the creative power of the Holy Ghost. Do consider the growth of those feet. Consider where his feet have been, how they have been marked. Pray consider where they are now, what is under those feet, consider what is over them. Consider where his feet are going to be; and consider in this world and age where thou art in relation to them and consider in the world to come and in eternity where thou shalt be finally in comparison to their position and status.

II

His Feet Uncovered

IN the doctrine and narrative of the old testament, not only the person but even the limbs of Christ were spoken of with unerring accuracy in the prophetic word so many centuries and even millennia before his advent. Therefore it is not surprising that his feet are mentioned, and even a part of them is written about from the primeval mists of dawning creation and the very period of the Fall itself. We find that the feet of the Lord are set forth in a metaphysical way, in a visionary way, in a typical way; they are set forth prophetically, in a way of imagery, and even didactically, and that recurring throughout the pages of the old testament from first to last.

For instance Boaz, of the seed of Abraham, the great-great grandfather of David, the ancestor and type of Jesus Christ, shows how sinners of the Gentiles find their place in relation to his feet, and are enabled to obtain an inheritance among them that are sanctified through faith which is in Christ Jesus.

Ruth—it is said—came softly and uncovered Boaz' feet and laid her down. How she could have been misunderstood. How men would have blamed her, and religious men at that, for what they would castigate as her immodesty. But Ruth uncovers Boaz' feet—for she dare not wake him with presumptuous familiarity—that when the cold arouses him he will enquire of her the meaning for her action. She trusts that such a judge as lies in the threshingfloor, as can discern

4

the wheat from the chaff and rest in his discrimination, will see that her interests are not carnal but spiritual, not worldly but heavenly, not of man but of God, not for self but in love.

And she is not disappointed—neither will his Ancestor disappoint my Reader—for he says: I will do for thee all that thou requirest. And what did she require but redemption, and interest in the sacrifice, a lot amongst the blood-bought people of God, her own place of rest with the saints in the Spirit of promise, an inheritance in the heavenly land; 'All that thou requirest'. She did not lie at his feet in vain. She came to him: do thou come. She lay still waiting upon him: do thou likewise. She lay in the dust at his feet: so do thou— and he shall do for thee all that thou requirest: 'I will redeem.'

Redemption is particular, and general redemption is a ludicrous and self-contradicting error. The Redeemer came forth to redeem the family of God and all those who had already been chosen into the family by an eternal election were acquired by the price of his precious blood and procured when Christ came into this scene—into the 'threshingfloor'. As with Ruth, the family relationship has been before engendered as now redemption has been once secured. Let the seeker sue humbly for such a redemption, such an interest, and lie low and lie long, till he whisper 'Daughter be of good cheer, thy sins be forgiven thee.' 'I will redeem.'

Ruth would not act presumptuously. She is so discreet and reverent. When he wakes it will not be due to her direct action. That is right, is it not? How different from those who speak to him so familiarly today who think to be on first-name terms with him, as though he were not both LORD and CHRIST. However, actually they do not speak to him at all but only to a figment of their emotive imagination, which they call 'Jesus', but the apostle calls 'Another Jesus'. Ruth, however, found her Lord in the only way in which he discovers himself to the seeking soul—in answer to tremulous awe, to meek reverence.

5

She uncovers his feet. Doubtless she waited long hours: what was she thinking? Wondering, trembling; at the darkest hour what doubts would assail—would he wake in time? Would he be furious? Who did she think she was? Oh! What doubts: but 'Fear not my daughter, I will redeem.' Take courage, seeker, and lie at his feet all night if need be, and though the world laugh thee to scorn: he will redeem in the morning.

And this despite the difficulties so much greater than one imagines that lie in the way. What a legal difficulty lay in Ruth's way of which she knew nothing: 'Howbeit', says Boaz, 'there is a kinsman nearer than I.' Boaz cannot act as kinsman-redeemer until one who has prior legal claim be legally dismissed! This other and first kinsman is not given a name in the book of Ruth, and he simply represents and embodies legal obligation. He is the law which came first. He is the legal obstacle that until overcome prevents the great Lover doing from his heart that which he desires to do, which is, save this poor woman: for even though Ruth was a foreign Gentile of polluted blood she was by marriage one of Boaz' distant relations and had thus contracted a relationship that bound the redeemer to give all that he had for nothing to pay her price and purchase her inheritance.

But another impersonal unnamed kinsman demonstrates that the law should come first: legal obligations must be met, the law must be magnified and made honourable. Lover and kinsman though Boaz was, should Ruth be married to him whilst as yet 'The first husband liveth'—so to speak from another figure—she shall be called an adulteress; but if the other first kinsman be lawfully dismissed she is free from that law. Grace taught her not to look for redemption, life or inheritance from the inexorable tables of stone, from cold legality, or from this impersonal embodiment of the law and what it could do: before, during or after that time, no, not to the law for redemption, help or advice—to Boaz she turns to solve this difficulty and all difficulties, now and always.

So Boaz meets the legal nearer kinsman in the gate—at the place of judgment—for Boaz knew the law so well. The redeemer knew that whereas the legal relation would redeem Ruth's mortgaged property, that relation would not soil his legal purity with marriage, for this embodiment of law knows nothing and wants nothing of union with disinherited Gentiles. Hence Boaz so ties up by law the two facets of redemption—inheritance and marriage—that the choice is both or neither. The unnamed kinsman will redeem the property, but he will not marry to raise up seed to Ruth's dead husband. Thus cold legality, so pure, so remote, so clean, will not descend to a moral union with a polluted sinner of the Gentiles freely to give life from the dead! Indeed it cannot stoop to pardon, much less to bear another's sin, and moreover it cannot give life because it is unable to reckon righteousness.

Boaz knew it. But the grace seen in Boaz was a justification-imputing, soul-saving, spirit-renewing, life-giving grace that raises the dead to give life from the dead. He lives, and reigns by grace through righteousness to give life to those who had lost both it and their right to a place in the land of promise. So Ruth lay at Boaz' feet till morning and did not despair. Neither do thou, Reader. Look what Ruth obtained: a Redeemer, a Redemption, and an Inheritance; and Boaz took Ruth and she became his wife, and they had a son, who had a son, and in sequence and in the end it was said 'Thou shalt call his name Jesus for he shall save his people from their sins.'

III

Straight Paths for his Feet

THE majestic dignity of the God of Israel was wondrously envisaged, and both his feet and path gloriously manifested in the mount when Moses and Aaron, Nadab and Abihu, and seventy of the elders of Israel went up after both the book of the covenant and they themselves had been sprinkled with blood. This is described in the twenty-fourth chapter of Exodus: 'And they saw the God of Israel: and there was under his feet as it were a paved work of a sapphire stone, and as it were the body of heaven for clearness.'

The heavenly way chosen and elect by the determinate counsel and foreknowledge of God, to whom all his works were known from the beginning, was absolutely clear—clearly of God, clearly of heaven—clear as daylight, clear as the body of heaven to those granted divine vision to see it. This way was set before the Lord's feet from before the creation of the world, and in God there never was any question, doubt, or shadow of turning; for the way of the Lord from the beginning was as an highway raised before him to tread out, under his feet as the body of heaven for clearness; neither could Satan, men, the world, history, nor any nation or event ever turn him from this course or take him by surprise, as though it were not foreseen or predetermined: so ineffectual was all this to alter the heavenly way clear beneath the Lord's feet, that for all the difference man and his will, the world and its ways, history and its vagaries made, they might as well not have existed.

This individual path for his feet was already precisely marked out and laid down when the law was given, and it was a path predetermined for the blessed divine man who was revealed at the giving of it; not that he as such gave the law, for strictly it was given by the disposition of angels and was ordained by them in the hands of a mediator, Moses. But it was then that this blessed man was here revealed, and a paved work stretched out in front of his feet indicating that the path was meticulously and particularly laid down in advance before him who should in the fulness of time purchase out a people by blood from the curse of the law, and redeem them from under that law itself.

Hence in Exodus from the beginning of the law there is a vision of the revealed Lord, which is another thing than two tables brought down from the mount having been disposed by angels at the command of the unseen Almighty. Nay, but by blood was an awe inspiring spectacle of the blessed person! man in God and God in man, and there he stood.

Before him was a path—paved and laid out for him to progress by steps—a heavenly way for his feet to walk upon. That individual marked out path stretches from the mists of eternity past, reaches through the creation at the dawn of time, and soars through the corridors of unfolding history. This is the way of the Lord prepared, this the making straight his paths, this is the bringing down of mountains and the elevating of valleys that the foolish and brutish utterly mistake and ascribe to luck, hap and chance. This is the highway traced out in its paving of the prophetic way laid down for the feet of the Son of man on earth, in time to enact what was before depicted in heaven from eternity.

IV

Blood upon his Foot

THE footsteps of the Lord's feet reaching down the halls of time are accentuated by the historic milestones of the books of holy writ. From Exodus at the giving of the law, the grace of our Lord Jesus Christ was envisaged. Tracing onward to Leviticus we read that Moses—mark it, Moses, the lawgiver —took the blood and put of the blood upon the tip of the right ear, the thumb of the right hand, and the great toe of the right foot of the priest of Jehovah. The priest that answers to the way of the Lord is made all bloody, because that is the way the paved work led—to blood. For this cause came he into the world—to bleed and die. This was what he heard in the secret counsels of the Godhead: the tip of his ear was marked by blood. That was the work the Father gave him to do: the principal digit of his working hand was bloody. And his feet went the way of Calvary, the way of the cross, the way of the blood-let sacrifice, for without the shedding of blood there is no remission of sins, and he came to save his people from their sins—there was blood upon his foot.

Thus the agonising cry, Psalm twenty-two, 'They pierced my hands and my feet.' I say there was blood upon his foot. This paramount truth appears in another form in the progress of the revelation in the prophet Daniel: 'His body also was like the beryl, and his face as the appearance of lightning, and his eyes as lamps of fire, and his arms and his feet like in colour to polished brass... .' Why polished? This had been well prepared, well rubbed down; this scores of prophetic hands

10

had smoothed with energy in the Holy Ghost, and repeated movements of the Spirit in the scriptures had made to shine the way afore prepared, symbolically set forth in the visionary feet of polished brass: great work had gone into the path 'for the Son of man goeth as it was written of him.'

And why brass? Because it is the metal of the brazen altar. It is the metal that marked the place of bloodshedding, of sacrifice, of substitution, as it was the metal that set forth the place of fiery judgment, of legal vengeance, of divine wrath. The great sacrificial altar was composed of brass and therefore always is to be associated with the substitutionary sacrifice of the Son of man and of the righteous though deflected wrath of God: not upon those who gendered it but upon him who bore it: thither his feet.

'His feet like in colour to polished brass.' So we see that the prophetic word of the seer's vision is a lamp to his feet and a light unto his path; lighting his way to the loneliest place in time and eternity, illuminating his steps to the most solitary journey in heaven and on earth, drawing his willing feet from the lambent paved-work of eternity and urging them towards the burnished Via Dolorosa upon the earth.

Oh! This loving man walked the steeps of the stairway to Calvary, to the brazen altar; up to where the brass burns red-hot: on, on to where the white heat of this livid inferno of elements all molten writhes and pulsates beneath the impression of shimmering incandescence, which in such blazing fire is all that can be discerned of the suspended brazen lattice-work: itself all aglow above the raging furnace. At the very brink he poises upon his feet; yet for this cause came he into the world.

Willing he yields, submissive he falls: the blazing coals of eternal fire erupt with shocking explosion to meet the Sacrifice, as the retaining lattice spreads to enmesh and impale the

11

agonising Sufferer for those long long seconds of infinite pain in compressed eternity till—stupendous sight!—till the volcanic fires of eternal wrath die out, till the fiery blaze is quenched, till the furnace is but dead ash, till the metal is cold: until legal justice is fully met, until the curse of the law fully uttered, until divine righteousness utterly vindicated, till 'IT IS FINISHED'.

So the vision of the feet of the risen Son of man in the last book of the bible leaps back through time to answer that of prophetic Daniel, for apostolic John tells the sight of feet that are no longer foretold as going, but are spoken of as actually having come out of the furnace of the brazen altar and been brought back from the dead to live for evermore. Revelation 1:15, 'And his feet like unto fine brass as if they burned in a furnace.'

The feet of the Son of man seen in the new testament therefore fulfil all the relevant prophecy, type and imagery of the old covenant and are the real limbs which hitherto were shadowed by metaphysical vision. That he has feet as such is a fact, and it is upon such a basis of reality that the solid and sound doctrine of the gospel is grounded. How wondrously have we seen his footpaths foretold and delineated with amazing lucidity in the paved work that reached back into the mists of antiquity: marking out from the very beginning in the third chapter of Genesis that 'the seed of the woman' should bruise the head of the serpent, and that the serpent 'should bruise his heel'—as it were to demonstrate that the feet of the Son of man should in the fulness of time stamp down upon the old enemy, Satan, to crush his head and destroy him, but that in the process the Lord's feet should suffer.

V

The Feet of the Son of Man

THE new testament opens to declare that these feet are coming forth into the world. How beautiful are the feet of them that preach the gospel of peace. The feet of Jesus were created uniquely by the Holy Ghost of the seed of the woman; these tiny feet of a little baby breached the womb of the pure virgin great with child –behold, I show you a mystery – and came via the travail of childbirth to lie straightway in the manger beside the exhausted but awed virgin mother.

Out of heaven, out of eternity, and out of inscrutable deity came the blessed Son of God; outwith eternal divine relationships ever before unknown and unrevealed in time, now to declare them in the body prepared, born with little feet no longer than his mother's finger. Oh what a staggering fact it is that he has feet, who was incarnate, who assumed human nature in the seed of the woman conceived of the Holy Ghost, God manifest in the flesh, very God of very God.

It is God the Son that came forth a tiny infant with frail feet incapable as yet of standing, much less supporting that little body. These feet grew as any other baby's feet grow. They supported him in boyhood and youth. In time they grew into a man's feet: he grew into manhood as really as humanity ever did so mature. How wonderful the man. His manhood is absolutely real. He is an actual man with feet that are distinctly his, his feet and no one else's with a footprint none other has: he is a real man, and what a man he is. He was

13

intrinsically divine, God himself, yet truly man; God the Father dwelt in him and yet he addressed God the Father in heaven. The Father could be in heaven, in him, in the Spirit and all absolutely one, indivisably one God—and this man could say not only 'I and my Father are one', but also standing upon his feet on earth declare at the same instant: 'Even the Son of man which is in heaven.'

None can explain these mysteries and no one ought to try, but they that believe know and experience their verity beyond the remotest vestige of doubt. These are they who have discovered his feet to be the place of mercy for sinners: for that which always has and always will confound scholastic doctors, and confuse theological professors, is as the body of heaven for clearness to poor lost sinners sick unto death: such come to him not to understand mysteries but believe them, not to get knowledge but to get saved, not to advance a career in divinity but to heal the ill of humanity, not to obtain a textbook subject for detached study with a view to the pride of life, but to weep all over his feet from a broken contrite heart a-trembling in a body racked with sobs, awed with amazement that he could ever love such an unworthy, vile wretch as oneself.

VI

At the Feet of Jesus

THIS profound truth is confirmed to us in the following passage: 'And Jesus departed from thence, and came nigh unto the sea of Galilee; and went up into a mountain, and sat down there. And great multitudes came unto him having with them those that were lame, blind, dumb, maimed, and many others, and cast them down at Jesus' feet; and he healed them: insomuch that the multitude wondered when they saw the dumb to speak, the maimed to be whole, the lame to walk, and the blind to see: and they glorified the God of Israel.'

In the context of this tremendous event in connection with the feet of Jesus, recorded in the fifteenth chapter of Matthew, the scribes and Pharisees had sent from Jerusalem a delegation. This party of religious authorities—so safe in the structure of the hierarchy—approach with all the hauteur of those who know their place and have one in the organisation, and with all the collective defensiveness of the insecure conformist towards the nonconformist man who scorns their whole system, and to whom both the need of the support and of the praise of men is less than small dust in the balance.

So they come to investigate this Galilean—and if possible bring him under proper authority now that he can be ignored no longer—certainly to point out his grave defects. They come with a question, not a direct criticism, a question; but it is all

15

two-faced, for they had already rejected him and the matter they raised was but to find occasion against him. But it goes against these hirelings for Jesus discovers their guilt, exposes their religious corruption, and turns away and separates from them. He then sets forth God's purpose in grace in taking up the poor Jewish remnant and going to the Gentiles. He becomes a blessing to a Gentile woman for faith.

Jesus returns to the sea of Galilee via Decapolis, coming to the territory of the outcasts of Zion. He was on the borders of the sea, among those that sat in darkness, right on the outskirts of Gentile country. Then comes this great multitude, to whom that established hierarchical organised religion was useless: hence to his feet came the outcasts, sinners of the Gentiles, the poor and needy, those whom God in Christ had chosen through salvation to be his church. This is that which commenced its existence at the feet of Jesus.

Now ascended, we see Jesus lifted up: 'He went up into a mountain, and sat there.' He is drawing all men unto him: 'And great multitudes came'—that is, unto his feet. As a result of his being sat down on high and exalted at rest, great crowds come to him or are carried to him and are restored, healed, forgiven and blessed. It is all grace: away from Jerusalem below, without tables of stone, and apart from works of the law, it is solely for the faith of poor sinners drawn to him consequent upon his ascension. Without doubt the afflicted of the flock and them that are afar off saw Jesus on high, set forth there in the mount for their blessing in his sweet compassion and almighty power unto salvation.

For in the ailments of those thus brought are seen the external indications of the internal sickness of man in the flesh: too wasted by deep-rooted disease to deceive themselves whole by assuming the cloak of religious externals. For these can neither walk, see, speak or use their strength; so helpless that unlike the whole—the whole that need only a bible to guide them—the sick are without strength even to hold the book, as without sight to read it: they need not only a preacher sent to teach but also a physician with power to unstop their ears. Nay, without rights or claims, hanging upon sheer mercy, cursed by law, without law, they fall at his feet or are carried there.

They cast them, note, at his feet. What a picture this conjures as of a rushing tumult casting, gasping, desperately falling, crowd upon crowd at his feet—Oh! If only that place be reached, all disease and death shall flee, bands will be loosed, and surely, as soon as they were there, swift as they were cast, he healed them all. And with what effect, 'They glorified the God of Israel.' They had not done so before because they were without vital experience that the God of Israel was such a God as this. It took the Son to reveal the Father. Religion without him—though it claim his name—was word without power, form without godliness, letter without Spirit, works without faith, reformation without regeneration, man without God.

Even in the old testament proper, God was hidden in the giving of the law and that behind thick darkness: thence beyond the veil unseen and intrinsically unrevealed, with even the prophetic shining of gospel light narrowed to the confines of the Jewish covenant; but the only begotten Son now has rent the veil, and in and from the bosom of the Father he has revealed him. Therefore at last by tracing his footsteps we see not merely how inadequate was the old covenant fully to reveal God in and of itself, but moreover how untrue was the representation of God by the scribes and Pharisees in completely misinterpreting what was truly to be known of him out of that old testament.

17

How contrary to the true legal testimony of God was the witness of the fallen religious system of men. So false was their view of the God of Israel that of Jesus in whom God's glory actually shone they said, 'Away with him, away with him, crucify him!' Yet the very difference between their theory of God—from their opinion of the law—and the actual reality of God himself revealed in his Son, was that which made them outraged against Jesus as false to the image of God! But however, it was this same distinction that seen otherwise by the outcasts, the strangers, the poor of the earth, caused these to glorify the God of Israel from the feet of Jesus Christ. The one nailed his feet to further what they considered to be the interests of legal religion, and the other fell at those feet because they had no religion.

What condescension in Jesus to permit such sinners to fall at his feet. Nay, himself to draw them thence with the cords of everlasting love. Such compassion; many waters cannot quench this love, neither can the floods drown it: if the wealthiest of all should give the total substance of his house for love it would utterly be contemned.

Love is all of God. Then what precedent thought, what immediate work, what subsequent delight in the deity, when behold! love's fruition is born and its responsive answer moves the heart as—in this example—there came one of the rulers of the synagogue, Jairus by name, and when he saw him he fell at his feet. What a blessed rustling of the ancient leaves of the book of life from the rim of eternity, what a joyful crying of holy angels from the lip of infinity, what a lambent burst of vast mercies from the edge of immensity, all brought to bear when poor Jairus in his extremity is made to see how cursed is the man that trusteth in man, but blessed is he that trusteth in the Lord.

'And when he saw him, he fell at his feet.' What love in Jesus, for to accomplish this humbling in Jairus. Omnipotence

18

had signified in heaven above, powers had trembled in space below, earth did obeisance in the firmament between, and hell cowered in the abyss beneath: but men perceived only, 'He fell at his feet.' Yet truly here is visible evidence of unseen things, of his having been set as a seal on Jesus' heart; divine love to Jairus being eternally as a seal upon Jesus' arm, now he comes to deliver him with a love as strong as death; and besides with Jairus himself prepared by the Spirit and providence of God for the tryst with a jealousy as cruel as the grave: the coals thereof are coals of fire, a most vehement flame. Yet verily, love cannot flinch the pain it must inflict to achieve its end, and it is plain in Jairus' suffering that many waters cannot quench love, neither can the floods drown it.

So love mysteriously works her purpose—yet however sanctified, exalted and glorified, his people neither ever forget their debt nor at all fail to remember their place, for the vault of heaven shall always ring with the cries of 'Thou art worthy', accompanied by the casting of crowns at his feet by the choicest of saints, world without end. And this is seen already in Mary who was ever found at the feet of Jesus. There never will be any in this coming glory but those who have sat at Jesus' feet all the journey through: blessed are the meek for they shall inherit the earth.

Mary—whom the law had once cursed—now sat at Jesus' feet. Mark the precious lessons she had learned! She sat at Jesus' feet, not Moses' feet; neither yet sat she with tables of stone at Jesus' feet, but at his feet; nor was she working, but at rest entirely. Neither was she there occupied with her religious reading—no, not even holy writ, had she such, for her posture declares as it were that even the word of truth must be laid at his feet. Not circumventing scripture—God forbid—but rather in a figure Mary yielded that word to him, as deeming it presumptuous in herself to do otherwise than devoutly wait on the Lord for the truth of it; not intellectually enquiring but devoutly seeking that from the holy scriptures his living presence might speak to her soul. Oh! lovely attitude. The sweetness of this place experimentally enjoyed is the most ecstatic in heaven and earth, bringing an exquisite bliss that makes the soul to cry—it is enough!

When Jesus passed by the country of the Gadarenes and healed the maniac, the populace went out to see what was done: what they noticed was that their swine had been choked in the sea; however, this enviable sign of national deliverance was not at all appreciated. Also they found the legendary demoniac who could tear asunder great chains, break in pieces the rock with the tremendous strength of the possessed, whose foaming countenance was awfully contorted with the terrible force of a legion of writhing demons swarming within, who had long struck with horror the countryside: this man! found 'sitting at the feet of Jesus clothed and in his right mind.' If men are in their right mind there they will be found; and, we see, there is no condition so desperate that men cannot be brought from thence to the place of the truly reasonable.

But perhaps one despairs of ever reaching so spiritual—so intangible—a place as the Lord's feet, in such an age as this? Yet it is written for present encouragement that once there were ten men which were lepers, which stood afar off, and they lifted up their voices and cried 'Jesus, Master, have mercy upon us.' A practice on their part vastly to be recommended to the despairing, and those who feel their soul is filled with blackness dense as the jet, hard as ebony. 'And they were cleansed.' And one of them when he saw that he was healed, turned back, and with a loud voice glorified God, and fell on his face at his feet giving thanks—he was a Samaritan. Then why not my Reader?

It is true that his feet are spiritually revealed now, but they are revealed to all them that seek him, and from however far off. Albeit now the Lord is revealed spiritually, he is just such a man as then; just as real, just as accessible to the poor and unworthy, just as piteously condescending to men of low estate, and moreover he still requires the afflicted to fall at his feet. Despair not, do not be put off by others, but rather be encouraged.

Refuse to be diverted from him himself by those who would lightly heal spiritual wounds and cover over one's true state before God with the cloak of ceremonialism, the vestment of formalism, the rags of priestcraft, the veneer of ordinances. Reject these that put presumption for faith, the text for the Spirit, the church for the Lord, india-paper for living experience. Renounce others who would superficially gloss over one's real condition with Pharasaical whitening, bolster false hopes with a Mosaic plaster, strap together what God never joined with some Sadducean splint, and support the wavering, tottering illusion with a pair of ecclesiastical crutches—at a price, of course, and only until that ancient preacher none can refuse, at the last bring with his chilly visit shocking and irreparable disillusionment: but too late. Away with it! The Christian faith concerns being brought to his feet personally. Jesus, now crowned Lord and Christ, is a wonderful man marvellously accessible to the poor and needy.

VII

The Pierced Feet

THE wounds in his feet demonstrate the crucifixion. Near
one thousand years from when the psalmist cried 'They
pierced my hands and my feet', and about five hundred years
after the prophet called 'They shall look upon me whom they
have pierced', he was sold for thirty pieces of silver as saith
the law and the prophets. He walked the way to Calvary as
perceived by the seer so long before; and as prophesied Isaiah
hundreds of years precedent, he was bruised in due course.
His heel literally was bruised, as wrote the ancient Moses in
the third chapter of the first book of the bible from the dawn
of time. John the apostle saw it all, tells of the fulfilment of
these and many ancient scriptures, and assures us his record
is true, as his consciousness and conscience bare him witness.

It was the chief priests, the elders of the professed people of
God, the scribes of the law and prophets, and those self-
appointed custodians of legal morality, the Pharisees, that
delivered Jesus with one consent unto the Romans: that
manoeuvred Pilate by political gambit, and checkmated his
clemency with diabolical subtlety, so that the Saviour was
taken, betrayed by the wicked, and delivered into brutal
Gentile hands—humbled and tortured—and so long as he could
bear the weight made to carry his cross along the Via Dolorosa.

Outside the gate of Jerusalem, at the place called Golgotha,
the soldiers nailed his hands and feet to the wood, reared the
stake, and hung him on the cross. Those wounds testify the

six long hours that he was suspended—impaled—upon the tree and hence they speak of the crucifixion of the flesh. His body was crucified. Whether they did so or not the wounds of the nails are not said to have caused bleeding. Blood was not shed till much later, from a different cause altogether, not without water, and all after death. But how many can tell us the doctrine of these distinctions?

These piercing wounds therefore draw the vision to his impaled body as such, and they who have an eye to see the stupendous sight see it—albeit veiled by darkness—as illuminated through revelation, and thus receive the true vision of Christ crucified. Such a seeing view comes not from the light of nature but rather is hidden deliberately from it by the darkness: no, this vision stands in the illuminating beams of the Holy Ghost alone, who divinely instructs the inmost soul that those in the good of such a revelation are crucified to the old legal rule that brought nothing but condemnation, a killing letter, a crushing burden, an unbearable yoke, a bitter enmity, self-righteousness, self-delusion, working sin, a curse, wrath, death, and a certain fearful looking for of judgment.

But a spiritual view of Christ crucified, pierced in the hands and feet of his substitutionary body, shows by that same body a full deliverance and discharge from Moses: in another—quite apart from his bearing the curse—the moral nature itself is hung up in the body thereof, and condemned to death by the Judge under the law. The crucifixion shockingly displays this, by the very elevation and transfixion of the lifted frame—the wounds in hands and feet show such awful substitutionary condemnation.

And the Spirit of truth will draw the eye of his people to look upon him whom they have pierced and see under the teaching of the Comforter such a sight of the Crucified as brings full deliverance from the law itself, light out of darkness and peace from enmity; they who see it experience a

23

spiritual manifestation that brings the love of God shed abroad in the heart, the ministration of the Holy Ghost, of righteousness, of life: nothing but a Spirit taught view of the crucified body of Jesus as such brings it, and his wounded feet therefore are precious in drawing our soul's attention to this invaluable truth.

What wonders also break upon the melted soul in a spiritual view of his precious blood, whether viewed upon the propitiatory in heaven on high, or sprinkled on the heart in the earth beneath: to the spiritual who view the work of Calvary what treasures the full vision affords. However, note well that his pierced feet in the first instance raise our eyes to Jesus' body as such.

Jesus Christ and him crucified, viewed perpetually and solely before the eye of faith, and intelligibly preached as immediately seen crucified amongst the saints—'before whose eyes Jesus Christ was evidently set forth, crucified among you'— brings in the truth that the law, moral or otherwise, hath no more dominion over the crucified with Christ; it brings in faith and makes the elect soul hang upon hearing. For without works, effort or striving, faith brings in a real holiness, a true righteousness; which so long as the demands of the law, or the law itself, were set before the people, was impossible; and so long as flesh strove to obey it, nullified faith and hence was without the Spirit.

By a believing view of Christ crucified, set forth in the simplicity of the apostle's doctrine and seen spiritually, comes the supply of the Spirit through the hearing of faith without the works of the law; the Holy Ghost came not from tables of stone nor ever will he, but the waters of the Spirit flowed from the smitten Rock and 'That Rock was Christ'. Out of no sight of the ten commandments, of moral duty, legal advice, but from a discernment that 'Out of his side forthwith came there out blood and water': thus issues the abundant flood.

A sight of the crucified Saviour brings deliverance from striving to keep the works of the law, and makes the soul to rest sweetly in the hearing of Christ; believing not working. It brings in the wisdom of God in a mystery to the poor and foolish of this world; it brings in a pathway shining more and more unto the perfect day: Christ crucified is a light to that path and a lamp to the saints' feet—as begun in justification so all the way to glory through sanctification of the Spirit and belief of the truth.

Only this view of him can bring just satisfaction in right-eousness met as to giving up the flesh, and solely that allows of rest in putting away all legal striving for false perfection. Certainly it brings a path of suffering and lonely separation, but not in vain: for it is in the weighty seed of God's sowing, and views a far more exceeding weight of glory yet to come. Such a view of faith brings the mighty testimony of God to that gospel centred in the knowledge of Christ crucified on mount Zion—utterly apart from mount Sinai—not in word only but in power also. To this view his feet direct us in that their being nailed demonstrates the crucifixion.

VIII

Behold my Hands and my Feet

THE fact of the Lord's feet argues the truth of the resurrection. Having been nailed to the tree, after six hours Jesus the Son of man gave up the ghost and died. Again after some hours, during which his dead body was hanging there in awful public display, it received the fifth wound out of which his blood was shed; not till then was his corpse taken down. Already rigid, unquestionably dead, it was a corpse—certified dead—that was carried away, wrapped in linen, wound up, and laid in a sepulchre hewn out of the rock. The entrance to this tomb was doubly sealed, and the body therein was as dead as ever dead could be as testified by the Authority and of many witnesses.

That cannot be questioned; what is asserted now is that on the third day Jesus the Son of man rose from the dead, and that he rose in the body in which he had died and which had been dead. That is the meaning of resurrection: it is not to do with the immortality of the soul but strictly and absolutely the rising of the body. That body, with the marks in it including the pierced feet wounded before death and rigid in death, was seen raised from the dead first by the women, then of Peter, of two others, of the twelve, and after that of above five hundred brethren at once, and not once only but for a period of forty days he was seen alive of them by many infallible proofs after his resurrection.

His feet argue the resurrection: very early in the morning of the third day after his burial the two Marys went to the tomb.

26

It was empty. The angel of the Lord in a vision directed the women to the disciples to tell them that Christ was risen indeed. As the two women went to tell the eleven of the angelic message, behold, Jesus met them saying, All hail! Then came they and held him by the feet and worshipped him. And no wonder. For what evidence: the feet they held had been pierced.

The two Marys put their hands on the identical feet that had been cold as marble in death for three days past: but now Jesus met them and they held him by those feet now throbbing warm and vital with life. Their hands—his feet. Their bodies this side of death—his body the other side of death. Four hands and two feet. Four hands that had never died but yet so soon must meet death—two feet that had risen from the grave and walked and should never again see death, world without end. They held *his* feet—what evidence! The pierced feet that were dead and are alive for evermore. And they held him by the feet and worshipped him.

But the disciples are astonished: they stagger at the resurrection. Appearing to them then, Jesus said, 'Why are ye troubled?' They believe him an apparition, a ghost: the immortality of the soul they can allow, yet the resurrection of the body is beyond belief. But Jesus replied, 'Why do thoughts arise in your hearts? Behold my hands and my feet, that it is I myself.' What will convince them? Seeing his countenance and his visage? No, but how were they swayed? 'Behold my hands and my feet.' Yet surely, they ought to have told it was he from his face alone? But these hands and feet argue the resurrection with a stronger reason, for they present the impregnable evidence of wounds all gaping wide: 'It is I myself: handle me and see; for a spirit hath not flesh and bones, as ye see me have.' That is it: flesh and bones. Without precedent, granted. Out of this world, truly. Past present reason, undoubtedly. But as one of our own writers well said, 'There are more things in heaven and earth .... than are dreamed of in thy philosophy.'

27

What a tremendous argument for the resurrection are his hands and feet. For Thomas said, 'Except I shall see in his hands the print of the nails, and put my finger into the print of the nails, and thrust my hand into his side, I will not believe.' And after eight days again his disciples were within, and Thomas with them; then came Jesus, the doors being shut, and stood in the midst, and said, 'Peace be unto you'.

Then saith he to Thomas, 'Reach hither thy finger and behold my hands; and reach hither thy hand, and thrust it into my side: and be not faithless but believing.' And Thomas answered and said unto him, 'My Lord and my God!' Jesus said unto him, 'Thomas, because thou hast seen me, thou hast believed: blessed are they that have not seen, and yet have believed.' And the belief in question here is the resurrection of the body. It is invincibly argued by his feet.

And if he arose upon his feet, then shall we upon ours. If by man came death, the death of the body, then by man also comes the resurrection of the body. If without argument mankind has followed Adam into death, then indisputably shall all duly follow Christ out of the grave. Indestructible matter, once wondrously created, shall be amazingly re-assembled, that had seemed so finally to dissolve in death. Ashes from the four corners of the earth; dust from the ancient crevasses of the everlasting hills; bones from full many fathoms deep; not to be created anew but reassembled again—small work for the Almighty who created into being from things that were not — thus shall be attested the age old saying of the wise man: 'For I know that my Redeemer liveth, and that he shall stand at the latter day upon the earth: and though after my skin worms destroy this body, yet in my flesh shall I see God.'

'Why should it be thought a thing incredible with you, that God should raise the dead?' saith the apostle Paul to Agrippa the king. Rather it is a thing to be thought far more incredible that God should not. Incredible that death be victorious, dissolution prevalent, darkness triumphant; inexplicable that chaos be perpetual, sin remain unanswerable, religion abide laughable; if any believe that, they are incredulous indeed. But credited or no, God hath given notice that the two feet of my Reader and those of his Writer shall walk the searing pavements of eternity; yea, even though death and dissolution intervene, yet risen then shall we tread out the destiny determined now: and that world without end. 'For God hath appointed a day, in the which he will judge the world in righteousness by that man whom he hath ordained; whereof he hath given assurance unto all men, in that he hath raised him from the dead.' So spake the apostle, but, 'When they heard of the resurrection of the dead, some mocked: and others said, We will hear thee again of this matter.' O to be in the spirit shown by the latter reaction.

IX

Worship at the Lord's Feet

BUT to proceed: further, the feet of the Lord the Son of man predicate ascension. For the ascension is that of the same body that was raised; no longer here precisely because ascended. For after that the Lord had spoken unto the disciples, he was received up into heaven, and now is set down at the right hand of God; that is where those feet are—pierced withal—by which he had led them out as far as Bethany: there, he lifted up his hands—wounded besides—and blessed them. 'And it came to pass while he blessed them, he was parted from them, and carried up into heaven.' Now he is on the right hand of the Majesty on high.

Thousands had been laid at his feet, tens of thousands; how many hands had held his feet, as their afflicted souls had sobbed out their plea in wretched and broken misery. None had been turned away. Clemency had met every cry at his feet. Now eleven men with some others and a few women watched those feet as they ascended up: for it was whilst—and as continually—blessing them that he was parted from them and carried up into heaven. What wondrous encouragement for those who seek him spiritually, to this latest moment; for verily there are those even after so long a time and at so late an hour that having sought, have found, and are experiencing today the blessedness of all who have not seen, yet have believed.

The unimpeachable apostolic witness is recorded further in the book of Acts: 'And when Jesus had spoken these things, while they beheld, he was taken up; and a cloud received him out of their sight. And while they looked steadfastly toward heaven as he went up, behold, two men stood by them in white apparel; which also said, Ye men of Galilee, why stand ye gazing up into heaven? This same Jesus, which is taken up from you into heaven, shall so come in like manner as ye have seen him go into heaven.'

This same Jesus: the same as seen in incarnation, that we have followed through his ministry, observed at the cross; marked as dead and buried in the tomb. This same Jesus that we have viewed in the resurrection: whom we then heard, and saw with our eyes, whom we looked upon as risen bodily from the dead—real flesh and bones—that our hands have handled. That is the point all along: this same Jesus—the same has gone into heaven. 'Is taken up from you into heaven.'

What a witness! From impetuously believing Peter, through cautiously contemplative John, to downright unbelieving Thomas: eleven men; several men; many women; five hundred brethren at once. Scoff one might, but it is all too much, and in the depths of the uncontrollable subconscious, the inextinguishable flicker bears uncomfortable subjective testimony with this certain objective record: 'And he that saw it bare record, and his record is true: and he knoweth that he saith true, that ye might believe.'

One might object—'But miracles are unknown: one never sees them: only those that ludicrously ape them, or persons childishly deceiving themselves.' Agreed generally; but these singular supernatural events accompanied the material presence of the Son of God. They mark the establishment of the new testament by its mediator, largely as was the parallel case with Moses and the old testament. Their absence now—as their comparative gradual withdrawal from the kingly period through Malachi to Matthew—is to be expected, not to be used as cause of doubting their ever having happened.

31

Man cannot always live his existence between the cosy walls of time, insulated by narrow but comfortable scientific postulations, and warmed at the hearth of the predictable certitudes of uniformitarian laws governing created matter. When time shall be no more, and when the elements of matter are dissolved, when insularity shall curl its blackened flakes of brittle fragment; then, then, attend more massive statutes, and loom hugely the vast spiritual verities so flimsily hidden by the transient wrapping. The tottering walls bulge with the tremendous pressures of eternity, and so soon the house of time shall collapse and the everlasting swell of eternal ages burst in, break down, and carry away the petty flotsam and jetsam of what we call time, apparently now so secure. But you have your Witness.

Be not staggered therefore by the apparent physical impossibilities of the ascension; the problem lies in the false assumption that no laws govern matter but those already observed in the context of time and creation. Palpably—at the least—this ignores the singular breaches into time of eternity, and ruptures into creation of the supernatural, that have in fact already taken place and otherwise been recorded in the old and new testaments.

These miracles were then faithfully set down by the scrupulously honest men that wrote of them: their record being received as true not only by the tens of thousands of the writers' contemporaries, but also by the thousands of generations since their writing. These previous generations had neither the temerity to question revealed divinity, nor the impertinence virtually to condemn as either liars or fools the most honest, intelligent, and—what is more—the most righteous men the world has ever known. Much less would they have done so in the name of either factual science or modern religion.

Since we are hearing of things outside of time that are eternal, outside of uniformitarian record and prediction that are supernatural, outside of the human that are divine, it is of necessity sheer folly to subject them to the criteria to which we submit things temporal, worldly, natural and humanitarian. Indeed the faculties must be humbled by conscious discipline not to rush in with heady conceit where angels fear to tread; and in fact, too often it is the lack of mental humility that is the negative problem of unbelief.

One cannot imagine the ascension because it concerns criteria beyond the scope of imagination: try to do so and it becomes ridiculous, if not idolatrous. The mentality and imagination has no precedent because the ascension is outside of laws and locations, conceptions and dimensions, as we know them. Also the mental equipment of the human—finite and temporal—is of itself impossibly inadequate to translate into its own terms what is infinite, eternal and divine. But to scoff the record of revelation because pride is frustrated, is not only the height of self-deceiving stupidity, it is the depth of self-destructive infidelity.

X

All Things under his Feet

CONSIDER therefore the apostolic testimony of the glory to which the ascension reached, and the elevated heights to which the Son of God ascended: 'God raised him from the dead, and set him at his own right hand in the heavenly places, far above all principality, and power, and might, and dominion, and every name that is named, not only in this world, but also in that which is to come: and hath put all things under his feet, and gave him to be the head over all things to the church which is his body, the fulness of him that filleth all in all.'

Observe that the glorious heights of the ascension to which the apostle bears record are seen in terms of the Lord's feet: 'and hath put all things under his feet.' This shows the elevation achieved in the exaltation of the Son of God and hence it is asserted that his feet predicate the ascension.

The passage quoted is neither prophetic nor typical, it does not refer to the Lord's feet in either a metaphysical or in a visionary way; neither is it a flight of imagery, but this soundly based doctrinal passage proceeds from solid and real facts, and refers the Reader to the same feet seen, held and felt in the resurrection. These are the feet that before death walked through the land of Israel; these are the feet that rose from the dead and after it again trod that very earth. It is actually those same feet referred to in the ascension, under which are put all things in heaven and earth, in this world and in the next, and which indicate the heights to which the Son of God has ascended.

This exaltation is over all creation, as was anticipated in the eighth Psalm, 'Thou hast put all things under his feet.' All else is beneath the ascension, including the very angels themselves: 'For'—says the writer to the Hebrews—'to which of the angels said God at any time, Sit thou on my right hand, until I make thine enemies thy footstool?'

That the Lord's ascension is until his enemies are made his footstool demonstrates that during the long period of this present age it is not the purpose of God to destroy his enemies, but is despite them to fulfil his work now in calling a re-deemed people out of this present world, and to do so in each succeeding generation, pending the destruction of all his enemies at the last day. The ascension is 'until' his enemies are made his footstool; thus till then he rules from on high by the Spirit and through the truth of the gospel, in spiritual Zion fulfilling the positive work of redemption in the midst of the raging but impotent enemies, and this the Lord does until the tremendous day of wrath dawns in fiery judgment at the last.

To return to this rhetorical question, 'To which of the angels...?' the writer is emphasising the difference in being as well as in the counsels of God between the Son of God and the angels. A distinction some would do well to observe more particularly. The created angels ordained the law which came by Moses the mediator of the old covenant; but the only be-gotten Son, God withal, which is in the bosom of the Father, is himself the revelation of the diety in the new testament. By angels men saw law, but, said Jesus, 'He that hath seen me hath seen the Father.'

The writer to the Hebrews is therefore showing this foolish people that were turning back from the new covenant to the law for help in religion, that by the law God was never revealed, but dreadfully hidden: the veil was unrent, there was blackness, darkness, unbearable words, a profound quaking, a prohibitive distance, and beyond it nothing but awful wrath.

And whether it be the renunciation of the new testament in favour of law, or the unlawful joining of law in any shape or form with the new testament, the old killing letter will bring in working sin, stirring rebellion, the ancient enmity; it will work wrath, threaten judgment, and bring despair: it will never bring to God. Hence to no angel was it said 'Sit by me!' But to the Son—who rent the veil, hid the tables of stone within the ark of his person, and sprinkled the propitiatory cover with the lifeblood of his passion—it was said, for himself and on behalf of that purchased people whom he had redeemed, 'Sit thou on my right hand.'

Such an exalted place as the right hand of God never could be given to angels, any more than men could experimentally enjoy its bliss whilst as yet law was in their view. But the Son magnified the law and made it honourable; far from making void the law—as did the legalists who called Paul the apostle, Antinomian!—the Son of man established the law: and as was seen in the shadow of the gospel under the law, he established it by lawfully hiding it in the ark, by honourably covering that ark, and by gloriously covering the cover. Blessed is the man that has learned what this meaneth. Blessed is he that reads and understands. To him hath the door been opened, and he has an answer to the ascension in his own soul, being drawn by the Spirit to the feet of the Lord in truth.

The significance of the comparison made between the Son and the angels in the epistle to the Hebrews, lies in the difference as such between the old and new testaments which were in fact ordained by the one and the other respectively. The apostolic doctrine is that if men will look back to the law for religious direction, it is to what was entrusted to angels for

36

a limited period that they turn; and if so now, necessarily they turn from the divine Son of God with the everlasting gospel who has the accord of heaven, in that he is set down at the right hand of the Majesty on high: not so the angels, which are seen as beneath his feet.

Those who ordained, and what they ordained, are seen as inextricable, and hence the comparison is not only between old and new testaments, but also between the angels and the Son of God. To angels pertained the ordination of the law; and to the Son, the gospel; these two are in total contrast, root and branch, and he who partakes of part of either, actually takes no less than the whole thereof and contrariwise has no part in the other. This is the reason that the Spirit contrasts the Son and the angels, by the rhetorical question, 'To which of the angels said God at any time, Sit on my right hand?'

Assuredly, such a statement could never be made to any angel, because it was made prophetically as conditional and consequent upon accomplished redemption. But the law under the express ordination of angels could not accomplish or finish redemption. The law made nothing perfect: it was added because of transgressions to curse them, not to effect forgiveness for transgressors to bless them; it brought to light imperfection, it cursed all under it to death, it hounded them through death to the judgment, and moreover it followed them through the tomb with the dreadful ringing echo of Ebal's curse. Holy, just and good the law is, true and necessary it might be, but because we are carnal and sold under sin, as a ministry it is nothing but condemnation and death; and would God exalt such a ministry to his right hand?

However, though the law made nothing perfect, the bringing in of a better hope did, and the accomplished perfection brought in through that hope, was the redemptive work of Jesus Christ at Golgotha's cross. No angel could bring in redemption for the law cursed sinners but did not forgive them; it condemned sins and would not remit them; it brought down wrath and could not bring propitiation. The better hope consequent upon accomplished redemption in Christ Jesus blesses sinners and does not curse them; it remits sins and does not remember them; it justifies the ungodly and will not condemn them; it propitiates wrath and brings in salvation; and all this not for this world only but for the everlasting glory yet to be revealed, and not for time merely but for the eternal ages yet to run, world without end, Amen.

Therefore, it is said, 'This man, after he had offered one sacrifice for sins for ever, sat down on the right hand of God; from henceforth expecting till his enemies be made his foot-stool.' It was said to that man to whom pertains this footstool; pray how would a formless angel either sit, or use a footstool? But this man was born with infant limbs, ran as a boy, climbed as a youth, walked as an adult, his feet developing in the normal process of bodily growth.

Jesus is that wonderful man, 'This man': the man who offered up one sacrifice for sins for ever, by which he secured the salvation of all the chosen people of God, whether then dead or alive or unborn: actually redeeming them at Golgotha by the offering up of himself, so as once for all to put re-demption in the past tense, and to do so eternally.

Think of that. How can he who is both priest and sacrifice, having been crucified, offer up the sacrificial oblation? How can this one man in a moment of time, extend his out-stretched arms to reach back to the creation, forward to the last day, withal standing in as substitute for so vast a multitude as all the elect people of God? How can he, with wounds all gaping wide, the pale ensign of death spread over his brow, how can this priest thus take the slain sacrifice which is himself, and lift thereof to God? I answer, because he is the everlasting Son, who by the eternal Spirit offered himself up in his humanity upon the altar of his deity, a divine self-offering as crucified man offered without spot by the Holy Ghost unto God and the Father. Oh what divine mysteries of the Triune God are here set before the eye of faith.

Yet how can unbelieving man, whose vision is all outward, and at that but a few score miles, peer through limitless space to these infinities beyond, withal into dimensions unknown? Oh! for that conscious, God-fearing mental discipline proper to the people of God, which the Spirit brings in when he 'takes the things of God and reveals them unto us, for the Spirit searcheth all things, yea, the deep things of God.' Therefore these things we speak, not in the words which man's wisdom teacheth, but which the Holy Ghost teacheth, comparing spiritual things with spiritual.

It is confirmed that henceforth therefore the Lord is expecting till all his enemies be made his footstool. Already they are under his feet: but although beneath his exalted authority, as yet he has not brought down his power fully to subdue them: neither is it the will of God nor the intention of the Son to do so till the last day. Then he shall bring down his foot—as with a footstool when the feet descend upon it over which hitherto they had hovered for a moment—then shall come to pass that which was written in the Psalms, 'That thy foot may be dipped in the blood of thine enemies.' And again, 'He shall wash his feet in the blood of the wicked.' Yet once more, 'Thou hast enlarged my steps under me, that my feet did not slip. I have pursued mine enemies, and overtaken them: neither did I turn again till they were consumed. I have wounded them that they were not able to rise: they are fallen under my feet.'

In furtherance of this doctrine the apostle teaches us, 'For he must reign till he hath put all his enemies under his feet. The last enemy that shall be destroyed is death.' That the apostle calls death the last enemy, implies other and previous enemies;

that he says the last enemy destroyed, leaves us in no doubt of the everlasting future of those who refuse rightly to submit to the authority of the King of Kings and Lord of Lords. As to those enemies, whether in the church or the world, whether in heaven or in hell, whether men or angels, all are enumerated in the book of the Revelation there being graphically described in a way of vivid symbolic imagery; the enumeration is then followed by an apocalyptic vision of all these enemies' perpetual but undying destruction.

'The last enemy that shall be destroyed is death': therefore no matter who or what has died, and no matter that the death were in the vain hope of the annihilation of the conscious being: since it is death that is to be destroyed, it follows that after death yet shall the dead live, and moreover at the last shall false hopes prove void, and the endless future ghastly indeed! For they who lived without Christ hoped that death would destroy all, and annihilate them; but they shall discover God true to his word, and what shall be destroyed and annihilated is not them but their death, and that not with a life span such as they had in this world before their view, but with an everlasting eternity before their rudely awakened and horrified gaze, world without end.

However, to those that are in Christ death is that enemy that stands between them and a better resurrection, a heavenly country, a new Jerusalem; death is that dark river between them and the promised land: a land flowing with milk and honey clothed in living green, and shined upon by the Sun of righteousness. These pilgrims and strangers on the earth, these heavenly-minded other-worldly people of God look past that last enemy to the day when the Lord shall put all things under his feet in power, when they shall enter the land at last; as the blessed of the Lord, entering by a better resurrection into the glorious inheritance prepared for them that look for his appearing.

And who shall stand when he appeareth? For the coming Lord will have all time unrolled and all mankind displayed before his face and beneath his feet. Then shall the righteous shine as the noonday sun, and then shall the wicked gnash their teeth. Then shall the false believer cry, 'Lord, Lord', pleading his gifts and miracles, doctrine and knowledge, confession and sacrifice—all to no avail! Then shall the foolish virgins be exposed not for the vast amount they had, but for the vessel of oil they had not—Oh! Then shall he put all, in the church and exiled from it, in the world and of the worldly, all in their just, righteous, and morally proper place in relation to his feet, death destroyed and world without end, Amen.

XI

His Enemies his Footstool

THEREFORE true wisdom—still crying in the gates and at the opening of the streets, but so neglected, or too late attended—plainly drops her doctrine as the rain and distils her speech as the dew: as the small rain upon the tender herb and as the showers upon the grass, she publishes unto men, and gives voice unto the sons of man, teaching them that like Mary, early they should be found at the feet of Jesus attending upon his word; then should they obtain that better part which would not be taken away from them, no, not in time nor in eternity.

As concerning the wisdom of presently bowing from the heart at his footstool, consider now what is beneath the Lord's authority: 'All principality, and power, and might, and dominion, and every name that is named, not only in this world, but also in that which is to come; and hath put all things under his feet.' Observe that the text is in the past tense, 'hath put'. It has happened. The fact that now we see not yet all things put under him is irrelevant. What we see is little or nothing. What is, his word declareth, and they that are taught of God are taught to know why what is, is not yet apparent in this existent world during the present age. But assuredly the reality is that all things were put under his feet; it happened historically at the ascension, and now is written history, a past accomplished fact: all things are now under the Lord's feet because they were then put there, so declares the apostolic record, and at the last it shall appear plainly how true and relevant is this tremendous witness.

The question which follows is, what are 'all things'? These things are in fact enumerated in the text as 'principalities, powers, might, dominion, and every name that is named, in this world and the next.' These titles in and of themselves basically refer to the structure and order of society, the governmental means of maintaining law and order; it is a question of the ranks and authorities in their relative stations in a proper society, the arrangement of government. As to the establishment of these positions, God has ordered society in structural strata: this is called the Economy, in which 'the powers that be are ordained of God'; whether they own God and are consciously submissive or not, their station is maintained by him, and moreover they are under the feet of the ascended Lord.

But what is generally neither acknowledged nor recognised is the fact that the greater part of this order in Ephesians stands in unseen heavenly powers: that is why the ascension must be so high in order for 'all things' to be brought under Christ's authority; as high as 'to God's right hand in the heavenly places, far above all principalities, powers, might and dominion.'

The common people often see the powers that be, in the visible social structure in their environment. These authorities are in contact with the echelons of central government above them; still higher ranks the inner cabinet and over all the supreme ruler: commonly seen or not, however, these offices are known because they are material and worldly. But what are not seen and are little known—at which scoffers mock for no other reason than that they are invisible—are the intangible spiritual dominions which soar above the world into the heavens. Here is the vast panoply of powers—whether alien or not—that are in the huge complex of a greater spiritual society far over and above the rulers and princes of the earth; yet notwithstanding far beneath the feet of the ascended and glorified Lord Jesus Christ.

Yet far above the powers, the rulers, the governments, the dominions of this visible economy, stand these invisible heavenly powers: unseen, but really influencing what is seen, even though the influenced are often unaware of the fact. These spiritual forces maintain the earthly governmental structures and rulers in their place so long as it is the will of God to do so. Thus it was said to Pharoah 'For this cause have I raised thee up, that I might show my power in thee': power displayed when God hardened Pharaoh's heart. And again, for higher reasons than either Cyrus or Persia, Cyrus existed; and God affirmed of him 'He shall perform all my pleasure'. Further it was said to Pilate 'Thou hadst no power at all, except it were given thee from above.'

It is from this high and invisible derivative source that sin is restrained, or not, in men and nations; from this that one is raised up or another put down, from this that revolutions are commanded, forms of government change, and the world alters, till history runs its course and the present evil age draws to a close.

Within this structure is that order of principalities, powers, and rulers of the darkness of this age, that are under the god of this world, the prince of darkness; but all these are far beneath the feet of him who is both Lord and Christ, and all must, despite their will, at present do his bidding and at the last be crushed beneath Christ's footstool. Yet many of these alien powers were appointed before their rebellion to uphold the world order, and not yet being put down perforce must still do so lawfully, and in this appointment are to be honoured and respected. It is not for men to 'speak evil of dignitaries'.

What the apostle reveals by the passage under consideration is that the economy of the world and age is not just a matter of human society on earth, nor of uncomplicated direct divine government. The whole structure has higher ranks above where earth's authority ceases, and it soars into the unseen and heavenly, ascending up to the throne of God. Moreover beneath the throne but within the heavenly economy there exists the fallen system, the 'present evil age', with 'rulers of the darkness of this world' and 'spiritual wickedness in heavenly places'. But even so, as to outward order, God upholds it for his purpose in the present age; none may over-step his bounds in heaven and earth, for law, order, and the decrees of God's counsel in an outward manner shall be observed, whilst spiritual and inward things run their course.

These strata of authority—the invisible ranks and orders of the economy—are upheld by God also for the maintenance of the cosmic structure. God requires from his throne that all powers must yield to the Almighty. Even the heavenly powers that were the origin of the Fall, whilst permitted to do their evil work, and hold fallen man in his self-willed rebellion against God himself, I say, even these must maintain a certain discipline and order as to history, society, and the cosmos: they themselves must exercise a certain restraint upon law-lessness. This curb, however, will be lifted at the very end and for a little season: then shall the truth of these words be plain to all.

In fine, although the world is a fallen one, the age evil, and the heavenly powers controlling it being those of darkness, still God is over all and requires restraint to be exercised for the fulfilment of his will and purpose in history, and among nations. This discipline upon principalities and powers is necessitated by the almighty power and authority of the Highest. This all powers are obliged to maintain: so that the Fall with its lawless rebellion—since the flood—can be exer-cised only within these permitted limits.

It is over all this economy that Christ rose, and is now by the Spirit through the gospel calling an illuminated people; he maintains in them a divine order in that simple and original true church. Moreover he will at the last supplant all the present authorities in heaven and earth, and in the world to come he will establish a new order from the throne, according to godliness. Hence it is said, 'In the fulness of time God shall gather together in Christ all things'—things, mark it—'both which are in heaven and which are on earth, even in him.' No principalities, or powers, neither might nor dominion, no angels, nor men, in that world to come, shall be in any wise in its economy or in its structure of government, but what are all in Christ. All is already under his feet: he has but to give the commanding word at the last day and for that, the Spirit and the bride say 'Come'.

Not within the nominal churches of organised religion as such, so as to be identified with them, but within that body gathered in the power of the Holy Ghost through the word of truth, is displayed wherever and whenever such a church appears under the preaching of the word, the intelligent and living embodiment of the truth that God hath put all things under the Lord's feet: the ascension has an answer by the Spirit through the truth in the congregation of the saints, and they feel and know his exaltation in fact. Spiritually it is to be seen in such a humble and lowly, living and regenerate church.

But not yet is that exaltation seen in the world, nor can it be discerned in the heavens. As to this world we see not yet all rule and authority put down. The old powers are still there, albeit beneath his feet. The economy is arrayed beneath him and subject perforce in the principalities, powers, lordships and dominions in heaven and earth: however, by and large—though not altogether—it is the enemies that are in these seats of authority, and they are not yet put down out of them. The Lord reigns over these powers, and they must do his will, and execute his commands who is head over all things, as all things are under his feet.

Yet a little while he permits the alien powers their place in the heavens, over the earth, under his feet: till the end of the age. Till then he reigns over them, but does not put them down. But in the end of the world he will rise, and tread them down, and overthrow from their places all powers, every enemy, and in the world and economy to come, put new powers that are in Christ in their places. All things in Christ shall then have come to pass.

However, now the discerning spiritually sense and doctrinally know Christ Jesus exalted as Lord, who once descended, and through death delivered his own out of the world—'I pray not for the world but for them which thou hast given me'— who was raised from the dead for them, and now appears in heaven in their behalf, whilst also reigning in them as united by the Holy Ghost below. He is head over all things to the church.

The Lord reigns over creation and will deliver it, and this reign is absolute and almighty, with all things fulfilling his merest gesture and inclination even now, and that for and in behalf of the poor little flock of his redeemed people below. However, it is true that because of the suffering way he brings his own as strangers and pilgrims, and due to the chastening and affliction that in love he often lays upon them, this reign is frequently most difficult to perceive at any given time.

Yet consider the dignity with which God has graced what the Lord deigns to call his church: 'All things under his feet, and gave him to be head over all things to the church which is his body, the fulness of him that filleth all in all.' The saints are called here, 'his body', and although this term is used in a mystical sense it is none the less a real one. Obviously the reference is not to his corporeal body in the personal physical sense of that body of Jesus in which he rose from the dead and ascended; but it is that body of called saints constituted his by virtue of the indwelling of the person of the Holy Ghost. For the Spirit proceeds forth from the Son and brings about union with him vitally and immediately, in the life and from the being of the Son. It is the body of Christ over which he—in his physical frame—is head in an authoritative sense, and in which he dwells by his life through the Spirit in a sense of vital union.

In this sense the figure 'body' is used to grace and dignify the church; and not without cause, when one considers the position of the body in relation to the feet. 'God'—says the apostle—'is the head of Christ', as in another place it is written, 'But when he saith all things are put under him, it is manifest that he is excepted, which did put all things under him.' God is stated to be over Christ's head, but in the amazing riches of his grace he has dignified his people in that, mystically, under the headship of Christ, the body of Christ is over his feet.

That eternal divine person who fills, indwells, and unites the body of Christ—the Holy Ghost—proceeds from the heart of the deity of the Father and the Son, and in that one divine essence is his distinct person; and since it is he that, proceeding forth from the Son, fills the people of God below, it follows from the divine intimacy of the union of the Spirit and the Son, that such a people must properly be called, The body of Christ. What dignity! The Holy Spirit who fills the church below proceeds out from the very heart of him under whose feet are all things subjected.

God is the head of Christ, and Christ is head over all things to the church, and all things are under his feet, save that body of which he is the head; for as taking us into union with himself in one body as his bride, he shares his name and place with us and it is in this sense that we are said to sit together in heavenly places in Christ Jesus. This is a great mystery, but I speak concerning Christ and the church.

As Eve was taken out of Adam, so in a figure the bride was taken out of Jesus' wounded side. Hence the body of Christ properly belongs above and as redeemed by him and united to him, the body of Christ by the Spirit is over the feet of the Lord not only actually but mystically. They therefore that were brought once to fall at his feet are now by one Spirit baptised into one body; and as of the body are elevated in grace to share his exaltation with him.

As joint-heirs with Christ and in union with him, we are graced with the position of our Lord; spiritually over the feet, but blessed be God and the Father, under his headship who is head over all things to the church, which is his body the fulness of him who filleth all in all. By grace the church which is his body is brought to sense all the height of the Lord's ascension and experimentally to enter into all the victory over the enemies, to enjoy all the rest of the Son, and to admire all the worth of the head.

XII

A Light unto his Path

FINALLY his feet postulate the inheritance. For this same
Jesus which was taken up from the saints into heaven,
shall so come in like manner as they saw him go into heaven.
And, given his feet existent, it must be so. After all, for what
purpose do feet exist? Feet are short flat-based, jointed exten-
sions at right angles to the extremity of each leg—remarkably
small considering their function—the sole purpose of which is
to keep the body in an upright stance by balancing it upon
the two platforms thus provided. When it is considered that
an erect body of weight up to some fifteen stone or more can
be supported on such small and irregular areas as the feet, it
is truly amazing; yet it is so that in perfect balance the feet
support the body in a vertical position, and moreover, carry
it along: for they are also for locomotion upon the earth.

That is the point: upon the earth! So his feet postulate his
inheritance. Surely it is not supposed that it is natural for a
man possessed of real, tangible, material feet, to be in the
heavens? Surely it is not thought that—drawn out though it
may be—this could ever be a permanent arrangement? The
point is that this economy, this present world, this earth, this
evil age—these are not good enough for the divine footprints
of this heavenly man. Yet the longsuffering of God draws out
the day, whilst scoffers mock: 'Where is the promise of his
coming?' And the grace of God calls out a people by the
preaching of the gospel from the midst of the world as time
rolls out its allotted span. Such a called people are manifest in

that they are not of the world, but look for, hope for, and long after precisely the same heavenly city, better country, and world to come as the Lord on high with whom they are inwardly united. So far, all these have died, and—though despised as fools on the earth, of whom the world was not worthy—have died in hope of a better resurrection.

The present reality of his feet declare the certainty of this resurrection, and thus the necessity of a world to come. Who can think that—in a real body of flesh and bones—the end of this resurrection is for him to remain permanently in the heavens? Is this the place for a body with feet? It is wings, not feet, that are made to move within space and are the feathery mode of airy locomotion. Feet exist for the body to stand on solid earth, to walk over the ground. They argue inheritance precisely because they exist; yet notwithstanding their existence they are not found upon this present sinful earth during the time of the course of this passing evil age. Therefore it follows of necessity from the fact of his risen body that the Son awaits a new heavens and a new *earth* wherein dwelleth righteousness, and in which—as the long, long wait over this present earth demonstrates—decay, corruption, mortality, are all swept aside, world without end.

The resurrection body is no feathery will-o'-the-wisp, as if the soul were ever intended to be a thing permanently separate from the body, escaped like some immaterial phantom genie materialising in vague smoky outline from out of some restricting lamp! Endless existence as a kind of shapeless ectoplasm? What an ignominious, inglorious, miserable eternity that would bring for man!

Nay, but the Son of God actually has two real and risen scarred feet of flesh and bone in the heavens at this moment; yet paradoxically this declares the abnormality of it all: in heaven? Then what a doom is pending this earth, what a judgment hovers over this city of destruction, as the sands of time drop their fast-emptying grains towards the bottomless abyss of eternity. Be advised then, Reader, that he shall stand in the latter day upon the earth, that new earth, that glorious delivered creation yet to be revealed: this for which the saints died in hope.

The resurrection is mysterious but it is real, it is not a phantasm with wings for the air, but a body with feet for the earth: yet not this present earth, but that had by inheritance in Christ for the meek, 'Blessed are the meek, for they shall inherit the earth.' That is it, the *earth*.

For such as are Abraham's seed by faith, there is a thrilling abnormality in that in heaven the waiting Son of God has a real body unsuited permanently to heaven, but raised for the everlasting inheritance to come. 'In whom also we have obtained an inheritance.' The creation itself groans waiting for this very thing, waiting for the manifestation —manifestation, mark it—of the sons of God, for the deliverance from the bondage of corruption, for the bodily redemption of the purchased possession. He who has the earnest feels the witness, for God has set to his seal that these things are true.

What we are now asserting about this blessed, divine, glorious, wonderful Son of God, man on the throne, at the right hand of the Majesty on high, is that his very body— there—declares that he is waiting. Waiting till time rolls off the spools of eternity; waiting till the solemn silence following the final tick of the ultimate moment of the last day declares that this vain world is no more; waiting until the day of the Lord comes as a thief in the night; in the which the heavens shall pass away with a great noise, and the elements shall melt with fervent heat, and the earth also and the works that are therein shall be burned up.

Notwithstanding this, the true—though now scorned and despised—people of God are looking for and hasting unto the coming of the day of God, wherein the heavens being on fire shall be dissolved, and the elements shall melt with fervent heat. How so? In that they, according to his promise, look for a new heavens and a new earth wherein dwelleth righteousness, and look for such things by way of a better resurrection. Wherefore—if ye look for these things—heed the apostle Peter, writing with great authority in his exhortation: 'Seeing ye look for such things, be diligent that ye may be found of him in peace, without spot, and blameless.'

Be advertised therefore that his feet shall stand upon the earth at the last, but not again upon this cursed soil, nor yet on that cleansed by the waters of the flood; what is raised and glorified does not, can not and will not come down upon this present earth. His feet were not raised ever to walk in this scene again: but they shall stand upon and walk the world to come, purged by fire, made anew without element of corruption or decay, and this is their assured destiny.

Yes! They postulate inheritance, these feet. Real feet, not for this world but distinctly for the glorious age to come, for him to walk in white with his redeemed and worthy saints, then raised with him to everlasting glory. Believe it, for his feet declare it, and to this his divine footsteps tend. Real feet are for a true inheritance.

This is what the disciples realised when they held him by the risen feet—soon to ascend—and worshipped him; for when those hands were taken away, and their grasp loosed from off his feet, so real were those limbs seen to be that the pale and lingering impression of their tightly gripping fingers bore eloquent testimony with the nail-pierced wounds: 'THE LORD IS RISEN INDEED.' And saith he, closing holy writ, 'SURELY I COME QUICKLY'. Amen. Even so, come, Lord Jesus.

JOHN METCALFE

53

INDEX

TO OTHER PUBLICATIONS

PSALMS, HYMNS AND SPIRITUAL SONGS

THE PSALMS

OF THE

OLD TESTAMENT

The Psalms of the Old Testament, the result of years of painstaking labour, is an original translation into verse from the Authorised Version, which seeks to present the Psalms in the purest scriptural form possible for singing. Here, for the first time, divine names are rendered as and when they occur in the scripture, the distinction between LORD and Lord has been preserved, and every essential point of doctrine and experience appears with unique perception and fidelity.

The Psalms of the Old Testament is the first part of a trilogy written by John Metcalfe, the second part of which is entitled *Spiritual Songs from the Gospels*, and the last, *The Hymns of the New Testament*. These titles provide unique and accurate metrical versions of passages from the psalms, the gospels and the new testament epistles respectively, and are intended to be used together in the worship of God.

Price £2.50 *(postage extra)*
(hard-case binding, dust-jacket)
ISBN 0 9506366 7 3

SPIRITUAL SONGS
FROM
THE GOSPELS

The *Spiritual Songs from the Gospels*, the result of years of painstaking labour, is an original translation into verse from the Authorised Version, which seeks to present essential parts of the gospels in the purest scriptural form possible for singing. The careful selection from Matthew, Mark, Luke and John, set forth in metrical verse of the highest integrity, enables the singer to sing 'the word of Christ' as if from the scripture itself, 'richly and in all wisdom'; and, above all, in a way that facilitates worship in song of unprecedented fidelity.

The *Spiritual Songs from the Gospels* is the central part of a trilogy written by John Metcalfe, the first part of which is entitled *The Psalms of the Old Testament*, and the last, *The Hymns of the New Testament*. These titles provide unique and accurate metrical versions of passages from the psalms, the gospels and the new testament epistles respectively, and are intended to be used together in the worship of God.

Price £2.50 (*postage extra*)
(hard-case binding, dust-jacket)
ISBN 0 9506366 8 1

THE HYMNS

OF THE

NEW TESTAMENT

The *Hymns of the New Testament*, the result of years of painstaking labour, is an original translation into verse from the Authorised Version, which presents essential parts of the new testament epistles in the purest scriptural form possible for singing. The careful selection from the book of Acts to that of Revelation, set forth in metrical verse of the highest integrity, enables the singer to sing 'the word of Christ' as if from the scripture itself, 'richly and in all wisdom'; and, above all, in a way that facilitates worship in song of unprecedented fidelity.

The *Hymns of the New Testament* is the last part of a trilogy written by John Metcalfe, the first part of which is entitled *The Psalms of the Old Testament*, and the next, *Spiritual Songs from the Gospels*. These titles provide unique and accurate metrical versions of passages from the psalms, the gospels and the new testament epistles respectively, and are intended to be used together in the worship of God.

Price £2.50 *(postage extra)*
(hard-case binding, dust-jacket)
ISBN 0 9506366 9 X

'THE APOSTOLIC FOUNDATION OF THE CHRISTIAN CHURCH' SERIES

FOUNDATIONS UNCOVERED

THE APOSTOLIC FOUNDATION
OF THE
CHRISTIAN CHURCH

Volume I

Foundations Uncovered is a small book of some 37 pages. This is the introduction to the major series: 'The Apostolic Foundation of the Christian Church'.

Rich in truth, the Introduction deals comprehensively with the foundation of the apostolic faith under the descriptive titles: The Word, The Doctrine, The Truth, The Gospel, The Faith, The New Testament, and The Foundation.

The contents of the book reveal: The Fact of the Foundation; The Foundation Uncovered; What the Foundation is not; How the Foundation is Described; and, Being Built upon the Foundation.

'This book comes with the freshness of a new Reformation.'

Price 30p *(postage extra)*
(Laminated cover)
ISBN 0 9506366 5 7

THE BIRTH OF JESUS CHRIST

THE APOSTOLIC FOUNDATION
OF THE
CHRISTIAN CHURCH

Volume II

'The very spirit of adoration and worship rings through the pages of *The Birth of Jesus Christ*.

'The author expresses with great clarity the truths revealed to him in his study of holy scriptures at depth. We are presented here with a totally lofty view of the Incarnation.

'John Metcalfe is to be classed amongst the foremost expositors of our age; and his writings have about them that quality of timelessness that makes me sure they will one day take their place among the heritage of truly great Christian works.'

From a review by Rev. David Catterson.

'Uncompromisingly faithful to scripture ... has much to offer which is worth serious consideration ... deeply moving.'

The Expository Times.

Price 95p *(postage extra)*
(Laminated Cover)
ISBN 0 9502515 5 0

THE MESSIAH

THE APOSTOLIC FOUNDATION
OF THE
CHRISTIAN CHURCH

Volume III

The Messiah is a spiritually penetrating and entirely original exposition of Matthew chapter one to chapter seven from the trenchant pen of John Metcalfe.

Matthew Chapters One to Seven

GENEALOGY · BIRTH · STAR OF BETHLEHEM
HEROD · FLIGHT TO EGYPT · NAZARETH
JOHN THE BAPTIST · THE BAPTIST'S MINISTRY
JESUS' BAPTISM · ALL RIGHTEOUSNESS FULFILLED
HEAVEN OPENED · THE SPIRIT'S DESCENT
THE TEMPTATION OF JESUS IN THE WILDERNESS
JESUS' MANIFESTATION · THE CALLING · THE TRUE DISCIPLES
THE BEATITUDES · THE SERMON ON THE MOUNT

'Something of the fire of the ancient Hebrew prophet ......
Metcalfe has spiritual and expository potentials of a high order.'

The Life of Faith.

Price £2.45 *(postage extra)*
(425 pages, Laminated Cover)
ISBN 0 9502515 8 5

THE SON OF GOD AND SEED OF DAVID

THE APOSTOLIC FOUNDATION
OF THE
CHRISTIAN CHURCH

Volume IV

The Son of God and Seed of David is the fourth volume in the major work entitled 'The Apostolic Foundation of the Christian Church.'

'The author proceeds to open and allege that Jesus Christ is and ever was *The Son of God*. This greatest of subjects, this most profound of all mysteries, is handled with reverence and with outstanding perception.

'The second part considers *The Seed of David*. What is meant precisely by 'the seed'? And why 'of David'? With prophetic insight the author expounds these essential verities.'

Price £6.95 *(postage extra)*
Hardback 250 pages
Laminated bookjacket
ISBN 1 870039 16 5

CHRIST CRUCIFIED

THE APOSTOLIC FOUNDATION
OF THE
CHRISTIAN CHURCH

Volume V

Christ Crucified the definitive work on the crucifixion, the blood, and the cross of Jesus Christ.

The crucifixion of Jesus Christ witnessed in the Gospels: the gospel according to Matthew; Mark; Luke; John.

The blood of Jesus Christ declared in the Epistles: the shed blood; the blood of purchase; redemption through his blood; the blood of sprinkling; the blood of the covenant.

The doctrine of the cross revealed in the apostolic foundation of the Christian church: the doctrine of the cross; the cross and the body of sin; the cross and the carnal mind; the cross and the law; the offence of the cross; the cross of our Lord Jesus Christ.

Price £6.95 *(postage extra)*
Hardback 300 pages
Laminated bookjacket
ISBN 1 870039 08 4

JUSTIFICATION BY FAITH

THE APOSTOLIC FOUNDATION
OF THE
CHRISTIAN CHURCH

Volume VI

THE HEART OF THE GOSPEL · THE FOUNDATION OF THE CHURCH
THE ISSUE OF ETERNITY
CLEARLY, ORIGINALLY AND POWERFULLY OPENED

The basis · The righteousness of the law
The righteousness of God · The atonement · Justification
Traditional views considered · Righteousness imputed to faith
Faith counted for righteousness · Justification by Faith

'And it came to pass, when Jesus had ended these sayings, the people
were astonished at his doctrine: for he taught them as one having
authority, and not as the scribes.' Matthew 7:28,29.

Price £7.50 (postage extra)
Hardback 375 pages
Laminated bookjacket
ISBN 1870039 11 4

OTHER TITLES

THE RED HEIFER

The Red Heifer was the name given to a sacrifice used by the children of Israel in the Old Testament—as recorded in Numbers 19—in which a heifer was slain and burned. Cedar wood, hyssop and scarlet were cast into the burning, and the ashes were mingled with running water and put in a vessel. It was kept for the children of Israel for a water of separation: it was a purification for sin.

In this unusual book the sacrifice is brought up to date and its relevance to the church today is shown.

Price 75p *(postage extra)*
ISBN 0 9502515 4 2

THE WELLS OF SALVATION

The Wells of Salvation is written from a series of seven powerful addresses preached at Tylers Green. It is a forthright and experimental exposition of Isaiah 12:3, 'Therefore with joy shall ye draw water out of the wells of salvation.'

Price £1.50 *(postage extra)*
(Laminated Cover)
ISBN 0 9502515 6 9

Newly Published Second Edition

DIVINE FOOTSTEPS

Divine Footsteps traces the pathway of the feet of the Son of man from the very beginning in the prophetic figures of the true in the old testament through the reality in the new; doing so in a way of experimental spirituality. At the last a glimpse of the coming glory is beheld as his feet are viewed as standing at the latter day upon the earth.

Price 95p *(postage extra)*
(Laminated Cover)
ISBN 1 870039 21 1

OF GOD OR MAN?

LIGHT FROM GALATIANS

The Epistle to the Galatians contends for deliverance from the law and from carnal ministry.

The Apostle opens his matter in two ways:

Firstly, Paul vindicates himself and his ministry against those that came not from God above, but from Jerusalem below.

Secondly, he defends the Gospel and evangelical liberty against legal perversions and bondage to the flesh.

Price £1.45 *(postage extra)*
(Laminated Cover)
ISBN 0 9506366 3 0

A QUESTION FOR POPE JOHN PAUL II

As a consequence of his many years spent apart in prayer, lonely vigil, and painstaking study of the scripture, John Metcalfe asks a question and looks for an answer from Pope John Paul II.

Price £1.25. *(postage extra)*
(Laminated Cover)
ISBN 0 9506366 4 9

The Trust announces the publication of a new title

THE BOOK OF RUTH

The Book of Ruth is set against the farming background of old testament Israel at the time of the Judges, the narrative—unfolding the work of God in redemption—being marked by a series of agricultural events.

These events—the famine; the barley harvest; the wheat harvest; the winnowing—possessed a hidden spiritual significance to that community, but, much more, they speak in figure directly to our own times, as the book reveals.

Equally contemporary appear the characters of Ruth, Naomi, Boaz, and the first kinsman, drawn with spiritual perception greatly to the profit of the reader.

Price £4.95 *(postage extra)*
Hardback 200 pages
Laminated bookjacket
ISBN 1 870039 17 3

'TRACT FOR THE TIMES' SERIES

THE GOSPEL OF GOD

'TRACT FOR THE TIMES' SERIES

The Gospel of God. Beautifully designed, this tract positively describes the gospel under the following headings: The Gospel is of God; The Gospel is Entirely of God; The Gospel is Entire in Itself; The Gospel is Preached; The Gospel Imparts Christ; and, Nothing But the Gospel Imparts Christ.

Price 25p *(postage extra)*
(Laminated Cover)
No. 1 in the Series

THE STRAIT GATE

'TRACT FOR THE TIMES' SERIES

The Strait Gate. Exceptionally well made, this booklet consists of extracts from 'The Messiah', compiled in such a way as to challenge the shallowness of much of today's 'easy-believism', whilst positively pointing to the strait gate.

Price 25p *(postage extra)*
(Laminated Cover)
No. 2 in the Series

ETERNAL SONSHIP
AND TAYLOR BRETHREN

'TRACT FOR THE TIMES' SERIES

Eternal Sonship and Taylor Brethren. This booklet is highly recommended, particularly for those perplexed by James Taylor's teaching against the eternal sonship of Christ.

Price 25p *(postage extra)*
(Laminated Cover)
No. 3 in the Series

MARKS OF THE
NEW TESTAMENT CHURCH
'TRACT FOR THE TIMES' SERIES

Marks of the New Testament Church. This exposition from Acts 2:42 declares what were, and what were not, the abiding marks of the church. The apostles' doctrine, fellowship and ordinances are lucidly explained.

Price 25p *(postage extra)*
(Laminated Cover)
No. 4 in the Series

THE CHARISMATIC DELUSION
'TRACT FOR THE TIMES' SERIES

The Charismatic Delusion. A prophetic message revealing the fundamental error of this movement which has swept away so many in the tide of its popularity. Here the delusion is dispelled.

Price 25p *(postage extra)*
(Laminated Cover)
No. 5 in the Series

PREMILLENNIALISM EXPOSED
'TRACT FOR THE TIMES' SERIES

Premillennialism Exposed. Well received evangelically, particularly through the influence of J.N. Darby, the Schofield bible, and the Plymouth Brethren, Premillennialism has assumed the cloak of orthodoxy. In this tract the cloak is removed, and the unorthodoxy of this system is exposed. A remarkable revelation.

Price 25p *(postage extra)*
(Laminated Cover)
No. 6 in the Series

JUSTIFICATION AND PEACE

'TRACT FOR THE TIMES' SERIES

Justification and Peace. This tract is taken from a message preached in December 1984 at Penang Hill, Malaysia. In this well-known address, peace with God is seen to be based upon nothing save justification by faith. No one should miss this tract.

Price 25p *(postage extra)*
(Laminated Cover)
No. 7 in the Series

FAITH OR PRESUMPTION?

'TRACT FOR THE TIMES' SERIES

Faith or presumption? The eighth tract in this vital series exposes the difference between faith and presumption, showing that faith is not of the law, neither is is apart from the work of God, nor is it of man. The work of God in man that precedes saving faith is opened generally and particularly, and the tract goes on to reveal positively the nature of saving faith. Belief and 'easy-believism' are contrasted, making clear the difference between the two, as the system of presumption—called easy-believism—is clearly shown, and the way of true belief pointed out with lucid clarity.

Price 25p *(postage extra)*
(Laminated Cover)
No. 8 in the Series

THE ELECT UNDECEIVED

'TRACT FOR THE TIMES' SERIES

The Elect undeceived, the ninth Tract for the Times, earnestly contends for 'the faith once delivered to the saints' in a way that is spiritually edifying, positive, and subject to the Lord Jesus Christ according to the scriptures.

The Tract is a response to the pamphlet 'Salvation and the Church' published jointly by the Catholic Truth Society and Church House Publishing, in which the Anglican and Roman Catholic Commissioners agree together about JUSTIFICATION. The pamphlet shows how they have agreed.

Price 25p *(postage extra)*
(Laminated Cover)
No. 9 in the Series

JUSTIFYING RIGHTEOUSNESS

'TRACT FOR THE TIMES' SERIES

Justifying Righteousness. Was it wrought by the law of Moses or by the blood of Christ? Written not in the language of dead theology but that of the living God, here is the vital and experimental doctrine of the new testament. Part of the book 'Justification by Faith', nevertheless this tract has a message in itself essential to those who would know and understand the truth.

Price 25p *(postage extra)*
(Laminated Cover)
No. 10 in the Series

RIGHTEOUSNESS IMPUTED

'TRACT FOR THE TIMES' SERIES

Righteousness Imputed. The truth of the gospel and the fallacy of tradition. Here the gospel trumpet of the jubilee is sounded in no uncertain terms, as on the one hand that truth essential to be believed for salvation is opened from holy scripture, and on the other the errors of Brethrenism are brought to light in a unique and enlightening way. This tract is taken from the book 'Justification by Faith', but in itself it conveys a message of great penetration and clarity.

Price 25p *(postage extra)*
(Laminated Cover)
No. 11 in the Series

THE GREAT DECEPTION

'TRACT FOR THE TIMES' SERIES

The Great Deception. The erosion of Justification by faith. All ministers, every Christian, and each assembly ought not only to possess but to read and reread this prophetic message as the word of the Lord to this generation, set in the context of the age. This tract is part of the book 'Justification by Faith' but contains within itself a message which is at once vital and authoritative.

Price 25p *(postage extra)*
(Laminated Cover)
No. 12 in the Series

A FAMINE IN THE LAND

'TRACT FOR THE TIMES' SERIES

A Famine in the Land. Taken from the Book of Ruth, with telling forcefulness this tract opens conditions exactly parallel to those of our own times. 'Behold, the days come, saith the Lord GOD, that I will send a famine in the land, not a famine of bread, nor a thirst for water, but of hearing the words of the LORD: and they shall wander from sea to sea, and from the north even to the east, they shall run to and fro to seek the word of the LORD, and shall not find it.'

Price 25p *(postage extra)*
(Laminated Cover)
No. 13 in the Series

BLOOD AND WATER

'TRACT FOR THE TIMES' SERIES

Blood and Water. Of the four gospels, only John reveals the truth that blood was shed at the cross. When it was shed, Jesus was dead already. With the blood there came forth water. But what do these things mean? With devastating present-day application, this tract tells you what they mean.

Price 25p *(postage extra)*
(Laminated Cover)
No. 14 in the Series

TWO NEW TRACTS

Women Bishops?

'TRACT FOR THE TIMES' SERIES

Women Bishops? This is a question that has arisen in America, but should it have arisen at all?

Read this tract and find out the authoritative answer.

Price 25p *(postage extra)*
(Laminated Cover)
No. 15 in the Series

The Heavenly Vision

'TRACT FOR THE TIMES' SERIES

The Heavenly Vision not only transformed the prophet himself, it became a savour of life unto life—or death unto death—to all the people.

'*Where there is no vision the people perish*', Proverbs 29:18. This is true. But where is the vision today? And what is the vision today? This tract answers those questions.

Price 25p *(Postage extra)*
(Laminated Cover)
No. 16 in the Series

EVANGELICAL TRACTS

EVANGELICAL TRACTS

1. *The Two Prayers of Elijah.* This tract, first printed in 1972, was reprinted in 1982. It shows the spiritual significance of the drought, the cloudburst, and the two prayers of Elijah. Green card cover, price 10p.

2. *Wounded for our Transgressions.* An evangelical message taken from Isaiah 53. Declaring the salvation of God, this is a tract intended to help those seeking the Saviour and his work.
Gold card cover, price 10p.

3. *The Blood of Sprinkling.* Taken from Hebrews 12:24 this booklet expounds the things to which the people of God are not come, besides those to which they are come. Obvious from the context, this is striking in the exposition. The saving grace of God is clearly preached in this evangelical tract.
Red card cover, price 10p.

4. *The Grace of God that brings Salvation.* An evangelistic address from Titus 2:12—originally preached in South East Asia in 1985—which brings home to the heart the work of God in the salvation of the sinner.
Blue card cover, price 10p.

5. *The Name of Jesus.* First preached to a Chinese congregation in the Far East, this pamphlet declares the reason for and meaning of the name given to the Saviour: 'Thou shalt call his name JESUS: for he shall save his people from their sins.'
Rose card cover, price 10p.

These tracts may be ordered directly from the Trust, or through Bookshops. If money is sent with order, please add letter post allowance.

MINISTRY BY JOHN METCALFE

TAPE MINISTRY BY JOHN METCALFE
FROM ENGLAND AND THE FAR EAST
IS AVAILABLE.

In order to obtain this free recorded ministry, please send your blank cassette (C.90) and the cost of the return postage, including your name and address in block capitals, to the John Metcalfe Publishing Trust, Church Road, Tylers Green, Penn, Bucks, HP10 8LN. Tapelists are available on request.

Owing to the increased demand for the tape ministry, we are unable to supply more than two tapes per order, except in the case of meetings for the hearing of tapes, where a special arrangement can be made.

THE MINISTRY OF THE NEW TESTAMENT

The purpose of this substantial A4 gloss paper magazine is to provide spiritual and experimental ministry with sound doctrine which rightly and prophetically divides the Word of Truth.

Readers of our books will already know the high standards of our publications. They can be confident that these pages will maintain that quality, by giving access to enduring ministry from the past, much of which is derived from sources that are virtually unobtainable today, and publishing a living ministry from the present. Selected articles from the following writers have already been included:

ELI ASHDOWN · JOHN BUNYAN · JOHN BURGON
JOHN CALVIN · DONALD CARGILL · JOHN CENNICK
J.N. DARBY · GEORGE FOX · JOHN FOXE
WILLIAM GADSBY · WILLIAM HUNTINGTON · WILLIAM KELLY
HANSERD KNOLLYS · JAMES LEWIS · MARTIN LUTHER
ROBERT MURRAY MCCHEYNE · JOHN METCALFE
ALEXANDER—SANDY—PEDEN · J.C. PHILPOT
J.B. STONEY · HENRY TANNER · JOHN VINALL
JOHN WELWOOD · GEORGE WHITEFIELD · J.A. WYLIE

Price £1.75 *(postage included)*
Issued Spring, Summer, Autumn, Winter.

xl

Book Order Form

Please send to the address below:-

		Price	Quantity
A Question for Pope John Paul II		£1.25	......
Of God or Man?		£1.45	......
Noah and the Flood		£1.90	......
Divine Footsteps		£0.95	......
The Red Heifer		£0.75	......
The Wells of Salvation		£1.50	......
The Book of Ruth (Hardback edition)		£4.95	......

Psalms, Hymns & Spiritual Songs (Hardback edition)

		Price	Quantity
The Psalms of the Old Testament		£2.50	......
Spiritual Songs from the Gospels		£2.50	......
The Hymns of the New Testament		£2.50	......

'Apostolic Foundation of the Christian Church' series

		Price	Quantity
Foundations Uncovered	Vol.I	£0.30	......
The Birth of Jesus Christ	Vol.II	£0.95	......
The Messiah	Vol.III	£2.45	......
The Son of God and Seed of David (Hardback edition)	Vol.IV	£6.95	......
Christ Crucified (Hardback edition)	Vol.V	£6.95	......
Justification by Faith (Hardback edition)	Vol.VI	£7.50	......

Tracts

		Price	Quantity
The Two Prayers of Elijah		£0.10	......
Wounded for our Transgressions		£0.10	......
The Blood of Sprinkling		£0.10	......
The Grace of God that Brings Salvation		£0.10	......
The Name of Jesus		£0.10	......

'Tract for the Times' series

		Price	Quantity
The Gospel of God	No.1	£0.25	......
The Strait Gate	No.2	£0.25	......
Eternal Sonship and Taylor Brethren	No.3	£0.25	......
Marks of the New Testament Church	No.4	£0.25	......
The Charismatic Delusion	No.5	£0.25	......
Premillennialism Exposed	No.6	£0.25	......
Justification and Peace	No.7	£0.25	......
Faith or presumption?	No.8	£0.25	......
The Elect undeceived	No.9	£0.25	......
Justifying Righteousness	No.10	£0.25	......
Righteousness Imputed	No.11	£0.25	......
The Great Deception	No.12	£0.25	......
A Famine in the Land	No.13	£0.25	......
Blood and Water	No.14	£0.25	......
Women Bishops?	No.15	£0.25	......
The Heavenly Vision	No.16	£0.25	......

Name and Address (in block capitals)

. . . .

. . . .

. . . .

If money is sent with order please allow for postage. Please address to:- The
John Metcalfe Publishing Trust, Church Road, Tylers Green, Penn, Bucks, HP10 8LN.

Magazine Order Form

Name and Address (in block capitals)

. . . .

. . . .

. . . .

Please send me .... current copy/copies of The Ministry of the New Testament.

Please send me .... year/s subscription.

I enclose a cheque/postal order for £ ....

(Price: including postage, U.K. £1.75; Overseas £1.90)
(One year's subscription: Including postage, U.K. £7.00; Overseas £7.60)

Cheques should be made payable to The John Metcalfe Publishing Trust, and for overseas subscribers should be in pounds sterling drawn on a London Bank.

10 or more copies to one address will qualify for a 10% discount

Back numbers from Spring 1986 available.

Please send to The John Metcalfe Publishing Trust, Church Road, Tylers Green, Penn, Bucks, HP10 8LN

All Publications of the Trust are subsidised by the Publishers.